MW00943433

This Belongs To:

____

Designed by: *The Blank Book M.D.*

Made in the USA
Coppell, TX
17 February 2023

12993430R00111